TAKE A LOOK AROUND

TAKE A LOOK

AROUND

Photography Activities for Young People

JIM VARRIALE

THE MILLBROOK PRESS
BROOKFIELD, CONNECTICUT

*Thanks to Lloyd and Michael Albin, Gail and Joe Espinosa, Peri Jacobson,
Christine and Max Sarry Varriale, Larry Alper, George M. Nicholson, and
to every camper who believed photography would be fun.*

FOR MAX

Photograph on page 2 and book design by Jim Varriale

Library of Congress Cataloging-in-Publication Data
Varriale, Jim.
Take a look around : photography activities for young people / Jim Varriale.
p. cm.
Summary: Uses projects to introduce various photographic concepts, including
shadow and light, camera angles, composition, action, and more.
ISBN 0-7613-1265-X (lib.bdg.)
1. Photography—Juvenile literature. [1. Photography.] I. Title.
TR149.V37 1999 98-32431 770—dc21 CIP AC
Published by The Millbrook Press, Inc.
2 Old New Milford Road
Brookfield, Connecticut 06804

Copyright © 1999 by Jim Varriale
Printed in the United States of America
All rights reserved
3 5 4 2

TO PARENTS AND EDUCATORS

The photographs you see in this book are the work of my young students. For eight weeks I taught photography at a children's summer camp in Connecticut. It was all new: The kids had never taken this sort of "class," and I had never been to camp.

These 35-millimeter images were photographed with twenty-dollar "point and shoot" cameras, which the students shared. When kids are learning to take pictures, more sophisticated equipment is unnecessary. The photography projects in the book are meant to be guidelines, designed to inspire a creative experience in children. Imagination (yours and theirs) is encouraged. More technical information, if needed, is widely available elsewhere (see the reading list at the end of this book). Here, the focus is on keeping photography fun.

Although the text is written for upper-elementary and middle-school readers, the projects are appropriate for most age groups. Unfamiliar terms appear in boldface in the text and are defined in a glossary on page 31. Even pre-readers, with guidance, can become empowered explorers with a camera. For them, a new way of seeing is also a new way of knowing—about themselves and the world.

In the classroom (and in the living room) photography can provide a context for conversation. When we give young people a method for self-expression, we give ourselves another way into their lives.

INTRODUCTION

This book will help you to see things the way a photographer does. The projects inside will open your eyes in an exciting new way. By using these projects as a guide, you can have fun while teaching yourself about photography.

To start, if you don't have a camera, buy (or borrow) an inexpensive 35-millimeter (mm) "point and shoot" camera and read the instructions that come with it. All the pictures in this book were photographed with this type of camera. These **fixed focus** and **fixed lens** cameras teach you to photograph with your feet. That is, if you want something to appear larger in your picture, you move closer. If you want something to appear smaller, you move back. Moving around allows you to envision all of your photographic options. Another common feature of these cameras is a built-in flash. Be sure that the camera you select enables you to turn off the flash (you'll see why as you read on).

When learning about photography, it's a good idea to work in black and white. Black and white film will allow you to concentrate on the basic concepts of photography without the distraction of color. Try black-and-white film—color will always be there.

Every type of film has an **ISO number**. This number (also called the **film speed**) indicates how sensitive the film is to light. The pictures in this book were photographed with ISO 400 film. This **high-speed film** enables you to photograph without a flash in almost every daylight situation. For that reason, ISO 400 black-and-white film (in 36-exposure rolls) is recommended for the projects in this book.

A certain amount of light is necessary to make a photograph, but the quality of the light shapes the mood of a picture. As a photographer, you'll learn how light affects your pictures. A good way to begin to learn about light is by photographing in daylight. To see the full effect of natural light, be sure your camera's automatic flash is turned off.

After you **expose** a roll of film, take it to a photo lab (or a store) that will **process** black-and-white film and make you a **contact sheet**. A contact sheet shows every picture from a roll of film on one 8- by 10-inch (20-by 25-centimeter) piece of photographic paper. The pictures will appear quite small, so look at your contacts with a magnifying glass. Or you may want to see a small print of each picture—the way most people look at their color shots.

Once you have your pictures, choose your favorites and ask yourself: What is it about a certain photograph that I like? Does it make me feel a certain way? Did I capture what I intended to? Does the photograph succeed in doing what the project suggested? If it doesn't, do I like it for another reason? What reason? Study your photographs carefully, and then save them in an organized way. At some point you may want a larger print made of a favorite shot. Take pride in your photographs. Display them for others to see. Listen to the comments they inspire.

Printing your own photographs in a **darkroom** is both creative and great fun. It's best to take a class or have someone teach you one-on-one how to process and print in the darkroom. Traditionally, the darkroom has been where photographers finish the work they began with the camera. Today, electronic photography along with computer printing offer exciting new ways for photographers to create images. Photographs can now be created without ever using film or darkroom chemicals.

No matter what method is used to produce the images, photography will always emerge from the creative process of the photographer. That process is what this book is all about.

HOW TO USE THIS BOOK

Use this book as a resource for ideas—it will help to inspire your own. Study the pictures, read the text, and then try the projects. They are designed to help you explore the concepts discussed in each section.

The projects will help you improve the quality of your observations and the clarity with which you communicate them. It won't happen overnight. With time and practice the concepts in this book will come more naturally to you, giving you more freedom to create.

The photographs in this book were taken at a summer camp. Your photographs will show where you are—right now. You don't need to be anywhere else. When you're thinking about what to photograph, ask yourself: What interests me? What excites me? What do I see differently than others? What's most important is for you to begin.

So grab your camera, go outside, and take a look around!

photographer: Jamie Duneier, age 12

SHADOW AND LIGHT

The word photography *literally means "drawing in light" (from the Greek). Photographers use shadow and light as their medium, just as a sculptor might use clay. Begin to notice how light changes the way things appear.*

P R O J E C T

On a sunny day, have someone create "shadow shapes" for you to photograph. Shoot only the shadows that your partner makes. Note that shadows are longer when the sun is lower in the sky.

Photograph a portrait outside on a sunny day. Place your model in the shade of a building facing out toward the sunlight. This shadowless outdoor light generally compliments a person's appearance by avoiding the dark shadows cast by direct sunlight.

Continue the photo session by moving into the direct sunlight. Make several photographs of your model's face with the sunlight falling on it from different angles (to do this, have your model turn in a circle). Notice how the sunlight, falling on the face from varying directions, changes the person's appearance.

Look around for interesting shadows. Photograph only the shadow, then include the object or model that is casting it.

Photograph the same object (or model) in various lighting conditions, such as a sunny day, a cloudy or overcast day, or a foggy morning. Compare the results.

This mysterious image is a study in shadows. Sharp and well-defined shadows like these are cast in direct sunlight. Now take a closer look at this photograph—you may have missed something. Because the photograph has been turned 90 degrees, what appears to be a net across the middle of the picture is actually the shadow of the real tennis net at the bottom of the picture.

photographer: Jamie Duneier

CAMERA ANGLE

The position of your camera in relation to what you are photographing is the camera angle. You can dramatically alter the way things appear in a photograph by changing the position of the camera. The constant search for the "right angle" keeps a photographer's eyes (and feet) on the move.

PROJECT

Photograph a large object (for example, a car) outdoors from various positions. Shoot from both high and low angles. Notice how parts of the object will appear larger, and other parts smaller, as you change positions.

Photograph a portrait from a low "shoelace" angle and a high "bird's-eye view" angle.

While lying on your back on the ground, photograph a friend as he or she leaps over you. Note how this low angle makes your subject appear large and powerful. Have your friend practice leaping over you a few times before you take any pictures, to help prevent accidents.

Make something look completely different by photographing it from various angles. An example might be a person holding an umbrella shot from above, and then from ground level.

By placing his camera against the climbing wall, and beneath his subject, this photographer used an extremely low angle to create a dramatic illusion. Also, the photograph was shot as a vertical image (to see this, move the book one quarter turn clockwise), but it's shown here as a horizontal image. Viewed like this, the climber appears weightless—similar to how he might look climbing in outer space.

photographer: David Lloyd, age 13

THE FRAME AND SCALE

When you frame a picture in the camera's viewfinder, you are deciding what you want to keep in, and leave out of, your photograph. The size of each element within that frame is its scale.

Without film in your camera, frame an outdoor object from many different angles and distances. Notice how the object's size changes in the frame. Pay attention to which background elements stay in your frame, and which leave your frame, as you move around.

Change the "story" a picture tells by changing your frame. For example, have two friends chase one another in front of your camera. First, include just one friend in your frame. Now move back and take another photograph to include them both.

Photograph someone from many camera angles. Try placing different parts of the model's body in the frame in an unusual way. For example, you might ask him or her to put a foot in front of the camera lens so that it partially fills the frame, making it large in scale.

Make a model stand out in your photograph by creating a kind of "picture frame" around the person. Use an object that visually surrounds him or her to focus the viewer's attention. (Imagine someone being photographed through a tire swing.) Now move closer to frame them without using the "picture frame."

This photograph tells a story beautifully. With the ball caught in midflight between them, the soccer players are shown (in small scale) at the center of the frame. The huge net rising into a misty sky makes for a dramatic **foreground**, while pointing out the awesome job of the goalie.

photographer: David Lloyd

COMPOSITION

When you arrange the placement of all the different elements within the frame of your photograph, you are composing it. Think of fitting the light and the dark pieces of your photograph together like a puzzle to arrive at a finished whole. Experiment with unusual compositions to make your photographs interesting to the eye.

P R O J E C T

Photograph a scene that has dark areas in the foreground and light areas in the background. Try to see these areas as flat shapes. By changing camera angles—high, low, left, and right—rearrange these shapes in different ways.

Photograph a person, full length, in front of the horizon line (the line where the sky meets the earth). Adjust your camera angle—high and then low—to change the place where the horizon line passes behind the subject.

Photograph a scene that allows you to change the meaning of the picture by altering the composition. (Think of the two friends chasing one another in the previous project.)

This composition grabs our attention. The geese, shot from ground level, are photographed so that they appear in between the dark blades of grass. This makes them stand out against the white sky background. Also, by surrounding the sky with dark trees, the photographer leads our eyes downward toward the geese.

A SEQUENCE

Photographs seem to stop time. Each one freezes a moment. With a sequence of images you can show the passage of time and tell a larger story, much as you might write a series of sentences into a paragraph. By photographing a sequence of images you can show how an event unfolds.

PROJECT

Using a friend as your subject, photograph a series of actions that tell a simple story. Make up a beginning, a middle, and an end to your story. Before you shoot, draw the story on paper. (Filmmakers call these multiple drawings a "story board.") Your story may be funny, sad, or angry—whatever you choose.

Think of yourself as a newspaper photographer. Go out and find a picture story that you can tell without words. Shoot key moments of the action and then put together a sequence of images.

Photograph the progress of something being made or built. This might be a short-term project (the making of a sand castle, for example) or one that spans several days or months (the construction of a building).

This sequence could have been captured by one photographer, but in this case a few photographers asked the boy to jump into the water several times. Ask your model to repeat the action if you cannot photograph it all on one try.

photographer: Jamie Duneier

photographer: David Lloyd

photographer: Jesse Rosenburg, age 10

photographer: Jesse Rosenburg

ACTION

Think about the expression "actions speak louder than words." In photography, it's certainly true. The ability to capture an action in real life, by "freezing" a moment, is unique to photography. A camera can record movements (and moments) that people don't ordinarily see.

Photograph a moving object (for example, a bicycle or an automobile) by **panning**. To "pan," follow the object with your camera frame as it moves by you and shoot the picture while the camera is moving. In the resulting photograph, the moving object should appear frozen, or "sharp," while the background looks like a blur of movement.

While tightly holding onto your camera, photograph someone (in direct sunlight) as you run along with that person. Instead of looking through the viewfinder, guess what the camera will see as you extend your arm to take the pictures. Don't worry if the pictures turn out blurry, just try to capture the energy and emotion of the moment.

Imagine yourself to be the sports photographer for your local newspaper. Photograph a game between two teams of kids your own age. If possible, keep changing camera angles. Try to anticipate the plays and be ready to capture them.

A girl's love of swimming is captured here—we can't help but feel it. This great action shot is an example of what a photograph can do so well. By stopping the action at a moment of great emotion, the photographer enables the viewer to feel the excitement that the subject feels being in the water.

photographer: Monica Elson, age 10

THE MOMENT

Every action has peak moments. Often, there is one split second that communicates a movement or emotion. The camera is a machine specially designed for capturing moments. Your job is to recognize the best ones.

Have someone perform an action for you. Pick out the one moment that best represents the movement or emotion of the action. Photograph that one moment several times as the model repeats the action for you.

Shoot a scene with lots of action. It could be laundry blowing on a clothesline or any scene that moves. Study the movement and then photograph the moments you find most interesting.

Create a dramatic moment with a partner. Stage a picture that tells a story in one moment of action. You can use props, wardrobe, location, and a specific behavior to create your scene.

These boys are determined! That's clear from their taut bodies and looks of total concentration. Somehow, without actually seeing the arrows that the boys have shot, we "feel" the arrows in the air. The photographer has captured the intensity of their action in this one peak moment.

photographer: Willie Dreisback, age 12

photographer: Justin Director, age 12

GROUP PORTRAIT

As a photographer, you will be outnumbered by your subjects at times. Learning to relate to a group is part of your work. The camera will give you the authority to direct your subjects. Whether or not you choose to direct their actions will determine the nature of the portrait you are creating.

P R O J E C T

Ask some friends to let you photograph them. Have them look at the camera. Say this: "If you can't see the camera, the camera can't see you." Now adjust their positions.

If you want your group to react in a certain way (and all at the same time) it helps them to know when you are going to take the picture. Try saying: "One, two, three, shoot!" Practice this with the group.

Direct your group to change their postures. Ask them to look away from the camera. Photograph them from unusual camera angles.

Photograph a group in a location that says something about them (an example would be a baseball team in a dugout). Now photograph them in an unexpected place.

Pay special attention to how a group is dressed. Clothing gives us clues as to what people do—or who they are. Think of the baseball team in their uniforms, workers in their work clothes, or a gang in the street.

These girls are feeling comfortable with the photographer. Notice the different emotions being expressed here. The camera angle—at water level—lets the viewer feel close to the girls and their feelings. Notice the casual way the girls are arranged within the frame.

photographer: Sara Lewis, age 9

A PORTRAIT

Our natural curiosity about people inspires us to want to photograph them. To photograph the inner qualities of a person, pay attention to the visible clues that help to reveal him or her. Clothing, posture, facial expressions, behavior, and location all contribute to our understanding of who the person is.

P R O J E C T

Take a portrait of someone you know well and try to "bring out" an aspect of the subject's personality. Maybe you find the person funny. By telling a joke, and then photographing the reaction, you may capture what you are looking for in your photograph. Using what you have learned about shadow and light, camera angle, frame and scale, and other concepts, how else can you bring out different qualities of a person in a photograph?

Illustrate a person's different moods by having him or her change postures. Try not to rely on facial expressions, but rather on "body language." Have the person use his or her entire body to convey a feeling.

Who is this girl? What clues do we have? What questions still remain? We are drawn into this photograph partly because it cannot answer all of our questions about the subject. Sometimes that is good. While a portrait can often tell us a lot about its subject, it can also give the viewer an opportunity to be curious by not providing all of the information.

photographer: Amanda Garcia, age 14

MOOD

Photographs can speak to us in ways that words cannot. By creating a mood, your pictures can communicate feelings.

Create a mood in a photograph by using a concept from one of the preceding projects. For instance, try making a friend look powerful in a picture. Choose a camera angle that would help you to achieve your goal.

At the very end of a sunny day, when shadows are at their longest, photograph a subject or scene that evokes a feeling of loneliness, isolation, or sadness in some way. Think of ways to frame this photograph that would bring out such an emotion.

Ask someone to help you create a photograph that will make the viewer laugh or smile. Use as many techniques from the preceding projects as you think will help. As an added challenge, your subject must appear to be serious in this photograph—no smiles or laughter allowed!

This moody photograph invites questions. The boy's languid pose, under a shady tree, might suggest pure relaxation to some people. Others, seeing the dark shadows of the tree and the buses in the background, may sense another story. Is this boy homesick? Is he bored? What do you see? How does this photograph make *you* feel?

photographer: Peri Jacobson, age 15

FINAL THOUGHTS

Photography, like all art forms, is a personal thing. The more involved you are with your photographs, the more likely your photographs will involve others. It helps to photograph what you know and what you care about—some part of your own life.

Learning about photography is really learning about a new visual language. This language allows you to speak without using words. Think of your photographs as your personal statements. They can express what you choose to say.

When you allow your feelings to show in your photographs, you become a better photographer. And you give the people who look at your photographs the opportunity to know who you are.

SOME WORDS
PHOTOGRAPHERS USE

contact sheet—a sheet of photographic printing paper with the photographs from an entire roll of film printed on it. It is called a "contact sheet" because the film negative comes in contact with the photographic paper when it is being processed in the darkroom.

darkroom—a photography workroom used to process film and to make photographic prints. It is usually kept dark (except for specially colored lights) so that film and photographic paper are not exposed to ordinary light at specific times during the development process.

expose—To expose film, or to make an **exposure**, you press the camera's shutter release button, which in turn opens the shutter inside the camera. (Think of a window shade that opens and closes very quickly.) When the camera shutter opens—generally just for a split second—light from outside passes through the camera's lens, making an exposure on the film.

fixed focus—a term used to describe a type of camera lens that does not allow the photographer to change the area of focus. It is "fixed," and allows for a general area of focus.

fixed lens—a camera lens that is permanently "fixed," or attached to the camera.

foreground—In photography, the foreground refers to the front area of a picture or scene, while the *background* refers to the area in the back or rear.

ISO number (film speed)—The ISO number, printed on every film package, indicates the "speed" of the film. High-speed film allows for photography in most situations, even in low light, while a slower-speed film requires more light to make a proper exposure.

panning—the act of turning a camera to the left or right from a stationary position.

process—a term used to describe the stages of using chemicals to develop film.

FOR FURTHER READING

Horwitz, Margot F. *A Female Focus: Great Women Photographers*. Danbury, CT: Franklin Watts, 1996.

Hubbard, Jim. *Lives Turned Upside Down: Homeless Children in Their Own Words and Photographs*. New York: Simon & Schuster, 1996.

Johnson, Dinah. *All Around Town: The Photographs of Richard Samuel Roberts*. New York: Henry Holt, 1998.

King, Dave. *My First Photography Book*. New York: Dorling Kindersley, 1994.

Kostick, Anne. *My First Camera Book*. New York: Workman Publishing, 1989.

Price, Susanna, and Tim Stephens. *Click: Fun with Photography*. New York: Sterling Publishing, 1997.

Stokes, Edward. *The Photography Book*. New York: Scholastic, 1992.

Sullivan, George. *Black Artists in Photography, 1840-1940*. New York: Dutton, 1996.

Watts, Barrie. *Photography*. Brookfield, CT: Millbrook, 1994.

Zubrowski, Bernie. *Shadow Play: Making Pictures with Light and Lenses*. New York: Morrow, 1995.

ABOUT THE AUTHOR

Max Varriale

Jim Varriale has worked as a commercial photographer and director/cameraman since 1981. His lifestyle, portrait, and fashion photographs have appeared in major magazines worldwide, and he is the recipient of a 1997 Art Directors Club award for his photographs of schoolchildren. This book, along with *Kids Dance: The Students of Ballet Tech,* are his first books for children. Mr. Varriale lives with his wife, Christine Sarry, and their eleven-year-old son, Max, in New York City.